The 2016 Poetry Marathon Anthology

I0191095

Edited by Caitlin Jans

Poetry, Poetry Collections, Poetry Marathon
0123456789

Authors Publish Press
Bellingham, WA
Published November 18, 2016

ISBN: 978-1-942344-02-5

Dedicated to the participants in the 2016 Poetry Marathon

Contributors

Introduction

The Poetry Marathon is a yearly event where writers from around the globe write a marathon – 24 poems in 24 hours – or a half marathon – 12 poems in 12 hours. The goal is to write one poem per hour. All of this takes place over the internet, on the official website and blogs as well as a private Facebook group.

When I first thought of the Poetry Marathon, I imagined it differently. I thought of it as a personal challenge, one I would undertake and complete on my own. When I told my husband, Jacob Jans, about my idea, he surprised me by declaring that he wanted to write 24 poems in 24 hours, too. Not only that, he thought we should try to convince others to join us in our insane endeavor.

In 2011, the first year of The Poetry Marathon, we were not able to persuade very many people to join in. But those who did wrote some wonderful poems, and they convinced us to host it again.

Between the first official marathon and the second official marathon, I tried to do a marathon on my own – just me and my laptop. It did not go very well. The poems I produced were not very good. Part of the magic of The Poetry Marathon is the idea that no matter how far apart the participating writers are physically, we are all in it together.

I think this is one of the reasons that around half of the poets each year have been repeat participants. It is addictive. Once you have completed the Marathon you want to be part of that kind of creative insanity again.

The 2016 Poetry Marathon is the fourth official marathon. It was very international. Poets in Canada, Thailand, India, Australia, Malaysia, Trinidad & Tobago, Spain, Pakistan, South Africa, UAE, Philippines, New Zealand, Zimbabwe, Lebanon, Jamaica, Romania, and Hungary participated in the marathon along with those from the United States. That's even more impressive when you take into consideration that we all write during the same 24-hour period, regardless of personal time zones.

This year over 500 poets signed up to participate in either the whole or half marathon. Less than half the people that signed up were able to complete the marathon this year. All of the poets in this anthology did complete the challenge.

I love how this anthology reflects the diversity of The Poetry Marathon community. Not only from around the globe, they are from entirely different backgrounds. English is the second language of approximately a quarter of the contributors. Some of the contributors are teenagers, others grandmothers or grandfathers. The contributors to this anthology are also teachers, farmers, lawyers, scientists, doctors, students, and any number of other professions. For some, this is their first publication, for others their hundredth. I love how their words and their chosen subject matters reflect that diversity.

Caitlin Jans

Half Marathon Poems

Davita Joie

Night Watch

Granddad's slippers slap the hardwoods with purpose,
Rising and falling like a beaver's tail
He walks the halls, opening and closing doors
Counts heads in bed
Watches chests rise and fall

Danger comes in the middle of the night
Sneaks up the back stairs
So he sits at his kitchen table in the North
Clad in nightshirt and work pants and blackness
With a shotgun on his lap
Remembering the terror of the South

Ears pricked,
Dark orbs swaying like the swoosh of a cat's tail
Argus-eyed

Different States (a Haibun)

Perseid meteors blaze across a sky darker than I remember. These white flares in the night foreshadow morning light.

White and black seem far apart in North Idaho where Republicans with rifle racks on rigs rule and beer bellies and boobs bounce into bars.

My coastal town sports kayaks on pickups and the tone is softer, like rain bouncing from a puddle.

Having lived in both places I know that most everyone will help a stranger if they can. Maybe life is Halloween with different costumes in different states.

An osprey drifts by
black stripe frames piercing eyes
dark necklace, white breast

Kevin J. O'Conner

The Doors on the Right Will Open

You will step out onto the platform
into the humid embrace
of the summer afternoon

You will melt
as you melt into the crowd
of which you are a part

but from which you are completely apart

The streets of Shibuya
will suck you out of the station
and into the open air

Tokyo will scream at you
right to your face

You will smile
though you know she does not love you
she is always there for you

Secret Geometry

(after Edgar Degas, *Le Petit Déjeuner Après le Bain, Jeune Fille S'Essuyant*)

What were you thinking? Did you get tired, Edgar, of petty complaints?
That you should be a realistic painter of ordinary women/men at
work/play. Or ballet dancers at the grand opera or jockeys racing horses
at the tracks?

But you didn't listen, did you? Trusted the way you defied the old beauties
— the maid's head cut off by the frame, and the unrecognizable breakfast
she is supposedly holding for the young woman exiting the bath.

And there's nothing believable about the scratchy rectangle off to the left.
Fabulous colors, but certainly not a bathroom's working drapes.

Who cares? So glad you didn't listen to any critic but your own heart.

Glowing Night

We parked the jeep
and watched the moon rise over a black glass lake.
Only a few clouds,
glowing with the glory of moonlight.
The entire sky lit up with stars.
A universe-sized canopy of fairy lights.
The baby fell asleep
in her car-seat.
We watched
for shooting stars,
until
we
fell asleep,
too.

Maritza Martínez Mejía

Oatmeal in Heaven

A simple meal,
reminds me of early days,
uncomplicated mornings,
simple as oats.

Pour, mix, stir, and wait.
Nothing else.
Straightforward meal,
simple as oats.

I am preparing oatmeal,
my mother's breakfast,
unsophisticated woman,
simple as oats.

I miss her so much
every lone day.
Mixed emotion feelings,
simple as oats.

Sheila Sondik

Angst

stang me like a cloud of gnats

Blue Arcs

I learned in English Lit
water represents rebirth.
But what about skies
that wisp overhead,
bleached cotton curtains that
suffocate the scenery?
I discovered in geology
the sky comprises
illusion, gases, and a nitrogen blue
that arcs like Aryan eyes
while cataract clouds
scuttle.
Plath called it a bell jar
smudged with
cloudlike condensation
or the pants of seven billion
symbiotes.

Now I am the teacher,
and I know
humans build near water,
bracketing the coasts,
bright and viscous,
like Florida algae.
Two humans, pale statues,
frame our view.
their interpersonal drama propels
the narrative, Aryan arc
while a blue plaid sky
snaps overhead.
The wind whistles their song,
the sun crisps their soft, beige skin,
the ocean crashes into the margins,
drowning their violence
and poetic flow.

Sandy McLellan

Drifter

Tangled curls, a mop.
Dirty clothes, the same as yesterday.
Nothing kept, only left.
Into the classroom I go,
teased again, what fault have I?
Only parents, drifting from place to place.
Tethered, I too am drifting.

Difference

I see the moving cities
Flying vehicles
Running people
They seem to have a destination
I don't

I see the busy city roads
And streets
And lanes
Even at midnight and after
They seem to be going
I don't

I don't run
I wander at leisure
For I have no destination
Just a journey
I do

Acedia

Reflections After Reading Kathleen Norris's The Quotidian Mysteries

Acedia: Spiritual torpor or apathy; ennui
                          -American Heritage Dictionary

The monk lays down his scriptures
And I, my laundry.

The monk looks outside his window. A spider walks across the ledge.
He looks again.
Same spider. Same ledge.

I look at my phone. Still no interesting anythings.
And when there are—
Too happy. Too productive.

The Acedian demon prowls in our sigh.

The 4th century monk Evagrius said,

                    The Sun hardly moves
                         If at all
                    The day is fifty hours long
                         If at all
          I look constantly outside my cell to judge
            when the ninth hour comes—lunch time.

I look at the clock again
and I wait for—
My husband to come home,
the witching hour to begin,
evening routines, and then—
everything on repeat.

But I wait mostly to learn the abundant life
in the wash rinse cycle,
the monotony of bedtime,
the chopping of undesired vegetables,
the clean up and put away,

in the brushing of teeth
and the picking up of play things.

How do we learn to pray as we floss little teeth—
With spittle on our faces?
The daily holy.
The discipline that all mother monks put on.

Teri Harroun

The Death Tender

Her home was outside the village
near the stables
quiet, restful, separate.
She spent her time reading, or writing, or tending to her flowers.
She had a cat that liked to nap.

She was the death tender.
Summoned when necessary,
needed,
tucked away otherwise.

She arrived smelling of star anise
that left a taste on your tongue even after she left,
from breathing in, and breathing out,
the anointed scent of journey
beyond.

Her breathing whispered Pachelbel's Canon,
the one in D,
the parade dirge,
keeping everything moving along as it should, as it would.

The death tender shook out the thin veil
that wrapped itself around the room
so instead of haunting it was inviting
silvery wisps of blessed light peeking through.

She prayed in ancient prose to ancient ones who had long ago
slipped into the light.
An ancient light growing brighter
never extinguishing.
Bringing ancient and present together in one star,
the return home.

After death,
the death tender returned
to her own home
outside the village,
near the stables
for now,

knowing one day the ancient would pull her through,
to return to being
stardust scented anise.

Ashes

I lost all my good words
a long time ago

like ash from a fire.

Stay quiet when you
want to think. Real tears

are a useful way
of getting to a place

where life doesn't
measure up.

Rewrite those rarefied
moments and never stop

looking for what's not there.
That's where the magic is.

Note: This is a found poem composed from quotes from the movie, The Magic of Belle Isle

Stinky Guy

All good cafes have a Stinky Guy.
He sits at the counter.
Frayed plaid sports jacket,
A sweater under it in winter.
Carries a stained cloth bag.
Sits at the same counter stool.
Orders 2 scrambled eggs, 2 pieces of bacon and toast.
Reeks of the street,
truck exhaust, gutter filth.
Skin left to its own devices,
without water, soap, toilet paper.
Grimy fabric helps insulate other patrons
from his noisome frame.
Only the waitress gets close.
He gobbles and mumbles,
Holds his fork like a shovel.
He eats alone,
pays in cash and tips well.
No eye contact or acknowledgement.
We all like it this way.

David L. Wilson

Haibun

Praying mantis stood planted close to the floodlight, swaying rhythmically back and forth in the night. Why? Was it trying to attract a mate with this movement? Attempting to rouse prey? Warming itself in the bright light? I watched and studied and decided: It was entranced by the play of its own shadow.

eclipse without fear
what may be found in darkness?
the essence of light

Marie Moser

Another Cup

coffee is a poet's tool
served black
in a white cup
unadorned
without sugar
without milk
uncompromised
by love

Raven Kingsley

Like!

All hail almighty *like*!
Hold on to it for your dear life.

Be vigilant and watch your friends:
who *likes*, who doesn't, who pretends.

A *like* might save you from tsunami,
increase your sales of origami,
can save a child in third-world country,
refill a starving person's pantry.

A lack of *likes* will kill your day
and cloud your mood in sunny May,
or make a girl, who isn't *liked*,
commit (how shocking!) suicide.

All hail almighty *like*!
Hold on to it for your dear life.

For if you don't, then your "friends" may
find someone else to *like* their way.

Naida Supnet

To Bid and To End

The sun sets for a day's end.
The leaves fall down the bend.
The rains fall, when it can't hold,
to bid and to end is a move so bold.

The sun should exit so the moon could come out.
The leaves should fall and new ones will sprout.
The rains should fall to wipe away the tears.
Yes, to bid and to end will welcome new cheers.

If it is time for my life to take a final bow
I will walk gracefully and I will show you how
I fared in this world with my poems and my verse,
and enjoy your applause which I know ain't rehearsed.

So the life I have borrowed, I'll return to the Boss,
and I hope I could get a high-sounding "kudos".
Thanks to you, thanks to you, I have had a good one,
with my man, with my child, and my poems that are fun.

Kathleen Kidder

Silver Sneakers or No Copay

EeeeGads!
It's that time again.
Oh that I were
30 years younger
and knew then
how demoralizing
health insurance would
be for baby boomers!
I'd have stashed
away all my petty cash.
Now I know why
they called it "petty".
I'd have put more
pockets in my bloomers,
left room for
more than tissues!
There'd be nice
deep pockets.
Yes, pockets with
extra Velcro for
100's and 50's.
By now my piggy-bank
would rival any
bull on Wall Street.
Then I could
negotiate.
I would not
capitulate!
Oh, my!
What to buy?
Medicare Advantage
or a Supplement?
Advantage schmantage!
Who needs glitzy sneakers!
Supplement? I thought
they were vitamins and
I have a drawer full.
Who knew…
So, it's that time again…
What to do?

Shyami Nazzaro

Breastbone

Do you have a spare breastbone?
Mine was shattered,
by the light of the moon,
under a canopy of stars.

I drove my Jeep
to the far end of the lake,
looking for you,
tasting the glory I would know
when our lips met.

Was it panic that set in,
when I saw you outlined in silver?
We'll have to use it, because no other word has been invented
to describe that flying apart.

Angst: The White Man's Burden

"Angst: a feeling of deep anxiety or dread, typically an unfocused
one about the human condition or the state of the world in
general"
"a feeling of persistent worry about something trivial"
(Oxford Living Dictionary)

Black folks
I'm telling you
Ain't got no time for no angst

We know what scares us
And it's up close and personal
Focused
In our face
Making us spitting mad

And scared

Folks too busy surviving
And striving
To prove we matter
We got something real
To fear

We keep our hands up
We are the human condition
We keep the cameras rolling
We are the state of the world

We are your angst
Because you don't think
We matter

Seeking Land

Everyone wants a home, but I'm afraid to call anywhere home when Muhammad Ali says that the rent you pay on earth is the service to others.

I want to plant.

I want to farm, to grow a little fruit tree.

I want to paint the walls and dig in the dirt as far as the eye can see, but wait… who owns anything, not me?

Pearl S. Buck knew that "The Good Earth" was more than about a home to call one's own. It was the land.

The Irish writer still echoes in my mind from college… many a family struggle to own the land under their feet.

"A condo is fine, but what about the land?"

"No matter how plush, or technologically advanced, no matter how high it reaches in the sky, how can a penthouse match the profound feeling when you put your hands in the dirt of a home on the land that you own?"

Langston Hughes and Lorraine Hansberry knew and made us all think deeper when we read the book and saw the play, *A Raisin in the Sun*. "To own even the dirt under your finger nails," a friend once shared, … "is worth something when you can call it your own." The value of owning a home is not something new.

Even Dido and The Cinematic Orchestra knew how hard it can be to build a home and no longer put your life for up for rent.

"Everyone deserves the chance to plant his roots in the ground." I hope I get this chance to plant a tree.

Walk Away

I could lay in your arms till my dreams fade away
Watch the stars fall from the sky with you
Never question a thing
I could be the perfect wife for you
If I wash my flaws away
Life would be so content with you
Within the image you create
But I would rather travel this life alone than to watch myself fade away
So I will say my goodbye now and walk away
                                    Walk away
                                         Walk away

Her Dreams

Her dreams rose past the
ceiling, for her dreams were made
of some migrations.

The End, I Wonder

I wonder if it's the end,
as I clearly remember the first time we met,
the first hug, the first kiss, the first dance,
still gives me butterflies in my stomach.
The first time I saw you,
the first touch of our hands,
the first glance into each other's souls,
still give me goosebumps.
I wonder if it's the end,
as the memories of us are still fresh as daisies.
I wonder if it's the end,
as you may be far from my eyes,
but not my heart.
I wonder if it's the end,
as I haven't given up yet.

Hologram Lover

Out of touch and out of sight, we seem so far apart.

Before, I am all eyes on you and now my heart drops and is broken in
half.

Dance with me hologram, to break your laser, to see you in person and
not in three-dimension.

Flirt with me, get my attention and we will make love in a coherent
beam of radiation.

Pinch me, shake, thrill me once again,

It is hard to carry on a civilized conversation in three dimensional
image, three is a crowd.

I want to get out of this kind of relationship, to avoid interference with
other electric conductor.

So sick and tired of being there for you, yet you are so far away, my
hologram lover.

Hoping the spark will come back and your fuse heart needs to energize.

Yes, I am totally falling out of love, every time we touched, you're more
like a ghost and as cold as ice.

I tried to be strong and keep the fight, but now, I give up. You need to
transform into a real person and not a hologram, lacking in
specification, to live with true intention.

Stop being a hologram with no backbone, you need to stand with strong
determination, to keep the marriage strong,

and of course you won't go wrong.

Ingrid Exner

An Unnatural Haiku

Your technobabble
leaves me unnaturally
disconnected from you now.

Joan Leotta

Woman with Dog

From the painting Luncheon of the Boating Party *by Renoir*

I am playing with my dog,
ma petit chien, Claude,
as our friend, Auguste Renoir, paints.
You think you know me
because you know the painting.
Ha! Look closely.
I am no model.
I am indifferent to Auguste.
To the others at the table.
To the food.
To the sunlight.
To you.

My husband ignores me
to flirt with a young woman
we just met at Renoir's picnic.
Our old friend, Auguste,
he takes it all in
with a quick sketch and
a splash of sunlit color
but I wonder if even he
really sees what is going on.
I am playing with
my dog and smiling.
How many will understand
it is because only
my precious pup
has compassion
for my broken heart.

John Sweeder

He Writes with His Actions

He writes with his actions.
Rising from his bed each morning
he grabs his coffee before
confronting his computer screen.

Rising from his bed each morning
he remembers fragments of dreams.
Confronting his computer screen
he begins typing intuition.

Remembering fragments of dreams
he wakes up abruptly
and begins typing his intuition
so he does not forget.

Lexanne Leonard

The Tower

It is a bit of a walk up to the tower
above green-green grass,
past the high school, past
the firehouse, next to the pool.
It's worth the trip.

Along the way stop signs post
for those who might not see,
those who need to slow down,
those who can't do it on their own.
Those who probably won't stop anyway.

Open space along the artery shelters
strays who in daylight hours rest,
under muted twilight hunt,
in sealed darkness feast.
All on the way to the invincible tower.

I course my tack, not straight and flat,
not always on steady pavement –
the approach my father instructed.
I feel curves and hidden wounded.
I leave before sun or wait until dusk.
I cede bright light to those whose
wrinkles tell of their own journey.

It is not the tower itself that tenures
the answer, high above, vista of the whole.
It is disruption of orange cones pushing
me aside, upheaval of sidewalk
buckling under pressure of rooted
tree, sudden movement within
stogie-spiked cattails.

It is revelation along the measure,
epiphany bursting open
as I somehow make my way
to the tower.

Lovely

That's what you said
As you whispered thoughts that have never come up for air
Drowning in your sentences
New and alive
Words melting icicles
Dripping wet in the sun

Good morning

That's what I said
And the newness of the day wrapped around us
A blanket covering our nakedness

Before Darkness

Dark nights in the town,
the moon wore a bridal gown.
The stars looked happy, twinkled, and smiled around.
The moon looked graceful but is missing now.
The nights are grey, only shadows dance. Why is the moon so shy?
Where has she gone, hidden in the sky? Citylights, buildings bright,
who has the time to sit, stare,
and gaze at the night sky? Who cares
if a star has fallen, the sky swollen?
Who cares? To search, to pass a warrant. Who cares? To feel the leaves
        covered in frost,
to think about the moon that is lost.
All comfy on our beds,
All happy in our inner mess.
Who cares to draw that curtain and look now?
To look at the sky and wonder how,
the earth goes round the sun or the sun follows you around.
They explained it a long time ago,
So we won't be curious anymore.
Moving yet not getting ahead, searching we will never comprehend,
Because all we have is a narrow one track mind.

Jo Eckler

Feline

Pointy feet navigating the ever-shifting landscape of the bedclothes.
She moves like a sundial around the house, keeping time, keeping warm.
Grace unfolding furry limbs.
The swish of sass in her tail.

Dead Poets Society

Despite the rain that day, I forewent the umbrella.
After everything, soaked clothes were the least of my concerns.
Watching them lower him down was the most painful thing I ever had to endure
but he'll never know it.
I lingered long after everyone else had left,
I only wish he did too.
Now, here I stand two years later
with no idea how I made it this far without him.
Sometimes, I think about jumping in after him
but then I realize worrying doesn't suit me.
I mean he brought us joy long before he took himself from us.
Why should now be any different?

Kathryn Trudeau

To Start at the End

Open. Widen. Rip.
Tear. Twist. Push.
A soul's first, first journey,
at the expense of another.
A mother's gift to her babe,
a gift unreturnable, unpredictable,
a present to create presence.
Love begets agony,
at its peak –
silence.
Time freezes, the world is created anew,
history forever altered,
countless lives to be altered, affected.
All because a mother's pain ceased.
But life began.

Valerie Wilson

The Clock Ticks

The clock ticks
its noise seeming
ever louder in the
darkness that is night.
The clock ticks
I can't sleep
therefore I wander
not only literally
but also in my mind.
The clock ticks
where is this taking me,
back to a painful time
that's never far from the surface.
The clock ticks
I can't sleep
I look outside at the silence,
stare at rooftops and streetlights.
The clock ticks
stars are hidden by cloudcover
I try to imagine them there
I can't sleep
The clock ticks
I close my eyes
but can't sleep
The clock ticks
The clock ticks
The bloody ticking goes on
and on and on.

Everyday Silence

Silence
touches my lips like a kiss remembered.
I sigh out, reaching
for which emotion to feel.
I miss the fullness
of knowing you are there.
Just the warmth of beautiful, strong palms
of a gentle hand holding mine;
the calm bliss of grounding
my comfort in the closeness
of you.

Where do I go now?
Enveloped by silence,
not as much as a whisper
of the warmth of yesterday.
It's too heavy,
the quiet.
I worry for how to carry it,
when all I want
is that simplicity,
that breathing in the presence
of the joy
of you.

It seems two dimensional now.
The everyday silence.

Saskia Lynge

When Night Descends

Rain melts the twilight sky as cresting waves pound the shoreline.
Wind lift me up, let me swim in the Milky Way, its raspberry
      sweetness on my tongue,
as dreams pass this dreamer by.
I caress the stars above, kiss the moon with tender lips, and bathe
in its silver luminescence.
The warmth of your hands cocoon my soul, as I dream of the one
      smiling back at me.
Dip me in your pools of beauty, remove my flesh, my crimson silk
      as sweet as liquid gold.
Whisper my name, and I will hear you.
Reach for me, and I will feel you.
Linger with me in the unknown, see me through the darkness and I
      will see your face.
Your loving smile, the warmth of your hands, seducing me back to
      life.

Twilight is gone, night descends and my dreams awake.
Memories taunt the familiar ache in my heart.
A chance was all it took, a chance I never got.
Shards of broken glass fill my cup, every clock's ticking hand
reminding me of time's finality.
I fought every seen and unseen war, and lost.
And then with my heart bleeding in my hands, I foolishly gave up
      destiny.

The cobalt sky descends, bleeding onyx into my memory,
as old dreams painfully awake.
Remove the light of your liquid silver, hold my breath, and grip my
      hand,
let me drown in your beauty.
With solar warmth burn me up, and birth me into another world.

Falling stars, fall with me.
Pearlescent wings unfold, fly me up into eternal night's bliss.
Venom of fantasy hunt me, take me, transform me.
Deity of all deities, make the impossible real, despite the dust that I am.
Congeal, bleed, flake, let me be what I dream of being.
Champion who will guide, I call to you. I wait for you.
Silent in the void, cocooned in the light that only you will see.

Dreams

The world is more difficult each day;
it's becoming more like a nightmare.
Humanity seems to be going backwards;
I'll leave the crabs out of this one.
There isn't good, new news anymore;
we recycle everything but recyclables.
The world is more like a bad dream now;
one we don't want to wake up from.
It's no dream; it's reality for most.
The only ones living in the dream
are the ones causing the nightmares.
Some people make nightmares out of dreams;
maybe they should make dreams out of nightmares.
One day they'll wake up
to the mess they've created,
but it'll be too late;
they'll wish they'd been dreaming.
Dreams open our eyes to better
things for our troubled world.

Jana Lapel

Cancel the Band, No Dancing Tonight!

Under the canopy
out at the lake
the wedding took place
though it was a mistake.

The Bride knew for weeks
that he was not the right guy
but she just couldn't handle
saying "goodbye".

She put on her makeup
and dressed up in lace,
repeated the vows
with a veil over her face.

Then after the wedding,
in front of the guests,
with the moon shining down
she was put to the test.

A pain in her breastbone
was cause for alarm,
panic set in,
She grabbed the groom's arm.

Here were these two,
in all of their glory,
nobody would guess
'twas the END of their story.

The Jeep was decorated
packed and ready to go
but the Honeymoon's over
'cause she finally said "NO!"

Sunshine

Slowly, long, pink fingers pull back the covers;
what a beautiful display.
Colored wisps blend,
caressing and creating soft curves,
across the morning sky.
Arising slowly, erasing the darkness into day.
The gray mist of dreaming fades in her fairest light.
As sweet, sensual sunshine bids adieu to the night.

Sensuous Elephant

Versatile giant, *the elephant in the room,*
piano in my head, *my sensuous corner,*
improvising tunes on patterns of black and white.
nothing memorable but the lovely mellow tones,
rippling arpeggios, majestic chords like cathedral chimes.
Such slow-passing long time since I played her.
Remembering why I need her, *she's mine.*
Her sound my body and soul in song.
Making lullabies, carols, hymns, arias soar.
Pink glow of consolation, release, healing peace,
joyful life fulfilled, *whole again.*
My sensuous beast.

Poorvi Singhal

Being Lost

I like being lost,
to not know
where the way ends.

I can stay blind.
Fear can't touch me.
The blind don't see scary things.

I can't hear,
the rules, the spiteful things.
You can't follow, what you don't hear.

I only have a voice,
singing is what I do.
I laugh at the order of the world.

The society doesn't bind me,
because I'm foolish,
and I like being lost.

Justin Broderway

To My Wildflower

She was like wisteria
Wild and free and purple
And she exploded into view
When summer turned to fall

How could anyone know
That I would love her most of all

What I came to learn
Is she was wild and free for sure
But she bloomed anew every morning
In the garden that earned my blue ribbon

She never fades or falls away
The sun never spoils her color
The rain never beats her down

She's my wildflower
Untamed by my gaze
Unaffected by my hand
Free to run and grow

In a world full of roses
I am ever focused on my wildflower
The view is never bland

Elisa Shoenberger

Body Politic

I was once accused of choosing to be different
because I preferred the gray in the ceiling of the world
instead of the joyful blue.
But we do not appoint the electricity in our brain
or the manner of blood as it rushes through our fingers.
My eyes chose the gray with the green green grass
as easily as my lungs chose air,
as if oddness were a decision.
I prefer the days where moving feels like swimming
or a constant embrace from stale warm breath.
I hide from the moments by the shore in the sun.
It's my body, not me.
If I only could luxuriate in the sun's embrace
or cheer with the blue and the green green grass,
but my manner is not appointed by me.
My nuclei have ordained it.
Thus I must follow
the gray days with the chartreuse trees.

Chapter 11: Ordeal

Alone on smooth hard stone.
No smell of pine.
No laughing moon.
No shadowed trees.

Where?
Nowhere.
Someplace like a mausoleum.
An altar's edge.
Opaque dark.
No telling how far down
down goes.

Wind like evil
prying fingers,
lifts and pulls,
pries and digs.
But, you must want to fall
to go over this edge.
You must give in.

II.

Forever or a day.
Pomegranate promise,
sitting on one corner
of this altar.

No dice.

III.

There must be a place
beyond.
There must be a way
through.
There must be a next
step.

No pomegranate promise.
No dice.

From the edge of this altar,
I leap.

Angel Rosen

No Tower

I remember the first time I was in a hallway with shrunken hips,
both my hips and those halls were white and red.
A decoration.
I remember the summer that I half disappeared,
holding tight to my bones,
so they wouldn't press out of my aching edges.
Another girl said she'd heard a rattle, she claimed it for herself,
but I knew it was me.
I wasn't excellent against the wind and water,
I just was. Eroded and slightly slanted. A leaning, but no tower.
No shrunken head, no voodoo doll,
Just a skinny girl with a too-big soul.

Mollie Doerner

Leaving Home

Never made a clean getaway.
Always left hairs in the sink
and unvacuumed spider carcasses
under the bed.

Never made it past the driveway
without smearing a tear through mascara
or running back for my coffee cup
left on the kitchen table.

Never forgot anything
that I couldn't ship or live without.
Stuff is only so important anyway
and memories don't weigh much.

Majestic Giants

The majestic giants were gracious today
and granted us permission to view
their ageless snow-capped heads,
good-natured hosts that they are.

Their arms, unapparent, rippled the cool air,
encouraged us to stay on the path,
made from the life they birthed,
good-natured hosts that they are.

Their tears of joy and fear of our company
filled a hole that gives life to us all
ageless time, serenity,
good-natured hosts that they are.

The majestic giants were gracious today
and granted us permission to stay.
May we count ourselves lucky,
good-natured guests we should be.

Pantoum Of Adoration

He is truly my medieval knight;
I seek him again this life.
Maybe it's a memory?
Or perhaps a book I read.

I seek him again this life.
He existed then, he must now!
Or only lives in a book I read.
How can I find him in reality?

He existed then . . .
The Universe knows my heart.
Show where to find him in reality.
I can feel his breath upon my neck.

The Universe knows my heart.
And shall always lead me there...
Where his breath is upon my face,
His lips upon my mouth.

Lead me there,
Put me in his strong arms.
His lips to my mouth draw me in...
And we become as one, again.

On Edge

I am on edge
waiting for something
to happen
filled with dread.
I question what festers
inside my head.
What could that be?

I am on edge
help me recall
what you have said.
I hurt inside
I want to remember
all the good
instead.
I am on edge
should I be
thankful I'm not
dead instead?

Pokemon Gone

These mindless hordes
have descended everywhere.
Roaming recklessly,
night and day.
In a craze to capture,
what, exactly?

Marathon Stream

breathe deep, exhale, now write
poems, poetry, fingers typing
words that make sense, words that are silly,
words that resonate, palpate and pulse
to ramble with sentences, free from constraint
let the muse flow unfettered, she's loose and unkempt
a creek's worth of water and words, creative juices
relax, let go, relent, forget
when sentences won't come, don't panic or tremble
just shake off the water and float through the pause
all is well, your best has been done
the race is half over, contest near complete
grateful when finished, content and connected
ready to swim once again in twenty-seventeen
you rock, you've done it, splash gratitude gushing
now shut down, rest your fingers, dry off, go to sleep.

Paul Sarvasy

At the End of the John Muir Trail

Sitting on rocks above the alpine lake,
our spare dinner eaten under
a canopy of high sierra sky,
we waited for the full moon to rise.

We planned at the end of our thirty-day trek
to climb the west side
of Mount Whitney and arrive on top
just as the sun rose.

Miscalculations of food supplies
left us with hunger in mind and body,
with all thoughts of glory abandoned.
Hail on top sent us back down to head home.

I turned twenty-one during the trip,
broke my glasses, lost weight,
and scrambled up Mount Sill.
Forty-five years later,
I still suffer flashbacks of
unconditional joy.

Full Marathon Poems

Alicia Martin

Not For Me

Some days I think I'll quit
and become a florist,
or a plumber,
or a chef.
Maybe writing just isn't for me.
Maybe I can arrange sweet peonies and yellow daisies better than I can
arrange 26 letters,
or maybe I can unclog pipes better than I can write through a block,
or maybe I can prepare a 7-course meal better than I can prepare a poem
for you to read.
Then I am reminded at 3 am, when the words are buzzing in my head,
trapping themselves in my mouth, cutting my tongue like a razor blade,
begging to be released on paper,
that I am a writer,
and there is nothing else out there for me,
and there never was,
or will be.

Shadow

I am here to return the bowl.
The door is never locked.
The house does not smell of cinnamon.
"Sketches of Spain" not on the turntable,
not in its red-yellow-black sleeve.
Sermon unfinished on the desk,
map open on the sink.
The closet is not empty.
The bedroom light glares
behind its square of frosted glass,
bedside floor polished
by knees and prayers.
The cat sits on the windowsill.
The window is open,
shade a yellow tattered scroll
raised halfway, or lowered.
The crow, itself a shadow,
is not in the cedar tree,
not on the clothesline
with its sagging bag of pins.
What have you given away?
The bowl is filled with apples.
How can I forgive your absence?

Three Ladies Lunching

A group of ladies numbered three
woke at dawn and went to tea.
They stirred into their china cups a shot of Irish whiskey.

They socialized until eleven,
talking politics and religion.
They ordered brunch and stayed 'til lunch and had a juice with gin.

One was rural, one suburban, one was from the ghetto.
One spoke alto, one spoke bass, and one spoke in falsetto.
They counted hours by the pint, each chased with amaretto.

Ere supper gone and evening come,
three ladies went home feeling numb.
They went to bed with buttered bread and a snifter full of rum.

Dream Girl Who'll Never Be #47: Florida Poolside

She
is a pale toothpick,
then crescent moon,
slender & seamless
in February sun.
I am gathering
her brightness
with slow unblinking eye,
how, for a moment,
she touches her own
fingertips & cascades
into herself, enveloped
like a torn napkin
in shattered water.
I know when her
eyes surface to mine,
clear the chlorine
with her hand's heel,
I will never
see her again.

Dragonflies

The dragonflies still buzz today
Flying so carefree and peacefully
Their wings dance on the breeze
Without a care in the world

Flying so carefree and peacefully
Reminding me of days in my youth
Without a care in the world
It was a much simpler time

Reminding me of days in my youth
I recall chasing dragonflies and laughing
It was a much simpler time
But everything is alright

I recall chasing dragonflies and laughing
Their wings dance on the breeze
But everything is alright
The dragonflies still buzz today

Michellia Wilson

Diggin' Taters

Nothin' smells better than
Indiana dirt,
bein' turned with a pitchfork,
tines sharp enough to pierce
clean through
anything that is in its path.

Taters exposed for the first time
to the summer sun,
warmin' the rich soil and
dryin' out the tan skins
of new taters that will soon
make the supper table.

We stoop over to sift through
black dirt to confiscate the prize
fruits of back breaking labor,
a family affair.

Nancy Pagh

Postcard to Richard Hugo
in Hot Springs, MT

Dear Dick. It's 1 a.m. Traffic's slowed, occasional. Sleepers cast into their lake of dreams. So much can happen in a life. A day. I wad so many up, throw them away. Watch movies cuz they're free. Read a book, write a poem? Occasionally. Lame. My writing needs a soak, PT. August 14, 2016. Who's ~~dreaming~~ writing now? I am.

frog's croak / needs oil / intermittently. —N.

Pamela Gerber

Acrophobia

When FDR declared the nation had only fear to fear,
he never had a gun to his head,
Ballistaphobia
never had a cobra hood opened at his bare legs
Ophidiaphobia
or strolled past the body of a jumper from a Manhattan 32 story
    high rise,
Necrophobia
the thump of the fall nearly lifting his feet off the ground.
But it wasn't then that a*crophobia* hit.

No, it was the carefree days of carnivals and Ferris wheels,
free from regulations and safety straps, not even for seats
that turned upside down with the slow-turning wheel.
I was five and my car mates were nine and ten, measurably
larger, taller than I so that the metal bar kept them in as
the wheel spun us upside down and then right side up,
me clutching with all my strength to keep myself inside.

*Thanatophobi*a. I had never heard the word in my five years,
but I lived my way through it many times since, perched on a ledge
peering down thirty floors into a postage stamp courtyard,
pondering the weighty sum of a life's body at its impact against the
    immovable.

Ardelle Hollis Ray

Cosmic Joke

65,000 years ago
a star's heart exploded,
spreading the message of its death
in neutrinos and fire.

My husband was the first to know,
but never knew he knew,
until the cosmic Humorist
decided to tell him.

He has wondered over the years,
yet avoids the answer.
What was the original joke
if he is the punch-line?

Transplanted

The creature darted across midday's blistering parking lot,
sheltering in the shade of one car, then another, as I watched
through the glass of a doctor's office door in my new home
        town, cool within.

It was lean and low to the ground, with tufts of fur rakishly angled
atop its erect ears, steel grey from a quivering nose to the tip of a long,
gorgeously full tail, an animal never to be imagined in this nearly
        treeless desert.

Its unmistakable silhouette, though skinnier and of a different color,
transported me in time and suddenly I'm homesick for green grass,
swaying walnut trees, and the evening rush of wind from an incoming
        storm.

Another hotfooted padding across the parking lot brought me back
        from sleek,
red squirrels scurrying and chattering through Indiana trees, to this
        pitiful,
flattened, grey cousin, straining to survive, a transplant to this dusty
        western town.

Conversations

Self contained
dramas abound,
I keep forgetting there are no limits,

from one drink to another and another,
conversation like satin,
I can not afford to slip

and then, like smoke I disappear.
Keeping the dragon that lurks within
on its chains.

Will Jackson

The Dining Room

My prismatic child eyes,
an older time to realize,
in a retrospective guise,
old farmhouse century.

A picture window facing west,
framing every family fest.
Eve's sun doth set the table best,
with sanguine filigree.

Jeweled leaves of summer waltz in space.
A tiny sparrow shows its face
too, in the winter fairy lace,
shimmers through for me.

Every memory glows with light.
Cousins smile and fill the sight.
Bid Aunt and Uncles all good night!
A happy memory.

Never since, have I found a place,
as warm and welcomed as this space,
my childhood gives a way to trace,
a kinder symmetry.

A happy memory,
shimmers through for me,
in sanguine filigree,
a kinder symmetry.

Amanda Potter

Taken Out of Context

Excuse me?
I can make my own
Excuses, thank you!

Pardon me,
for asking
How are you?

Despondent world
Welcome home!
Most, don't really care
Have a nice day!

Excuse me,
for having hope.

Jacob Jans

Counting

And one for the hours in grocery stores,
blackberries scooped over ice cream at home.

And two for Karina's delicate scones,
the many small crumbs I'd sweep off the floor.

And three for the train rides to Beacon, NY,
the gallery where we had a big fight.

And four for the hammock we slept in tonight,
our bodies so tangled, like tines on two forks.

And five for Church Mountain, the bird at the top,
the sunrise that woke us, the peaks gently pink.

And six for that staircase, my sudden instinct,
to circle down flight after flight, and to stop

and wrap my arms oddly around you,
not knowing how all this would come true.

Dark Days

Darkness slips silently, tight to the ground.
On cautious velvet paws,
a cat
is absorbed into the shadows
of an ebony hedge
which rustles
and is loosed
into dark air
and rough-winged flight.
A crow
rises
where
murky clouds cluster
in a brutish sky.
Darkness
flitting before me
above me
and beyond me.
Sometimes the darkness stays.

Callan Waldron-Hall

Synthetic Leaves

we make /leaves from silk/ and become gods
we make life out of /notlife/

--you think we can change the world

awaken the Emerald City?--

I tell you /I'm happy/ with what we've made
and twist together flowers for you but /you want the moon

to be green/ so you climb into a rocket
made from thorns but in space you lose speed / /

your rocket can't fuel itself as much as you
would have liked so /you change course for the sun/

and now /you have everything/ you need
but will get nothing you want

Joyce L. Bugbee

The Ivy

The ivy crawled up the chimney
sneaking into the cracks
where water found a way in,
and expanded.
The ivy crawled up the chimney
hiding behind the morning glories
that camouflage the damage
till bricks crumble.
Large chunks fall
bringing the ivy down too
until all that is left
is a pile of broken bricks
held together with ivy.

Haunted

When I think~
I think of you.

(and think of you i must)

I think about~
The way you looked.

(you last looked at me)

Survival Shelters

A white walled room holds only one bunk bed,
many bodies come and go,
families of two, four, six,

10 spaces available,
28 days to restructure your whole life.

Children's laughter phases out sounds of slammed doors,
a mixture of emotions fully expressed,
ambiance level has been set to safety,

children with brief friendships that last for their stay,
a mini-break for survivors,
not long enough to recuperate.

Trauma has made "our bodies tired".
Left over belongings of an abusive relationship:

a few toys for the children,
a diaper bag for the baby,
a duffel bag of clothes,
and a whole lot of maybe.

Those can be placed in the closet.
Welcome to our shelter.

Chanacee Ruth-Killgore

Caught in the Margins

Shuffled from place to place
by edict and form
in triplicate.
No one asks.
No one listens.

They're all on their way;
so many places to be,
so many important things,
more important
things to do.

He waits…

While discussions continue
about him,
around him.
Do they even know
he's sitting right there?

When did his years
become a mark against him?
When did wisdom fade?
When did senility
become assumed?

He waits…

At the center of discussion,
while pushed
to the back of the room.
So many voices speaking
on his behalf.

His best interests,

their best practices

discussed ad nauseam,
as time marches on
and all the while

…he waits.

Molly Hickock

Dear Santa Claus,

You selfish and outrageous capitalist.
You prey on hopes and dreams like
a leopard preys on the children whose
dreams and hopes you're built upon.
You fascist pig of a concept, deliverer
of jealousy and anguish every year.
Every year someone gets killed and
every year it's because of your values.
You teach children to be selfish.
To be poor is a crime and to be
rich is the only right way in your
eyes which glow only due to your
lies! Lies by which people lead
their own insignificant lives! Who
cares if they don't have enough to
eat, who cares if they are made of
sins? Either way, the Santa Claus
wins. You get more if you're rich
than if you are poor, rewarded for
no one's actions save the slaves
in sweatshops and factories
while mom and dad sip
glasses of black sherrys.
It's your existence that
perpetuates fear in a land
that is called 'free' or
fright in a child no older
than three! And you have
Absolutely no shame do you?
Well I'm through with you

Sincerely,
The poor kid

Hostage

i am the common enemy
of people who conspire to control me.
Sometimes in packs, sometimes alone,
i am hunted.
i recognize in their harsh eyes
the same quench for power, the same sick sin.
They lie, they manipulate me
with their half-truths.
If i expose them, they will stop
at nothing to tear me limb by limp limb,
so i back away, step by step,
and i retreat.
i have smelled embers of evil
smoldering in the hollows of their dark,
slithering, putrid intestines;
i suffocate.
i disdain the thin veil they wear
and quiver at the depths of deception
atop alabaster altars,
under heaven.

Yoni

I take leaves from my garden and fruits so sweet, I once cut an onion just to be honest with me, that there is pain in me, but I shaved back the thoughts that kept me... whispered my grandmother's words over the steam... "be a woman sweety, and you will learn this not by following me, but by being everything you were meant to be", the leaves turned dark green and my ancestors bubbled in the boiling water... even more steam drifted up upon me, I squatted over truth and my insides creamed, I passed through the feeling of gathered lives within me and let my yoni be sweet and bitter and lovely...

Paralyzing Flame

Darkness captured my soul.
    There wasn't any place to go.
The flame on my body was so strong.
    I could feel my soul numbing

with the worst pain my body could feel.
    It was captured with the darkness.
And my body couldn't get away
    from the flame.

I had to let the darkness over come me.
    I felt the flame surround me.
I was captured with darkness from hell,
    my screams inside.

I Couldn't escape the flame.

Sixteen

By the time we met
I was sixteen and ready for anything.
I had bargained away
my second virginity
to a friend's ex-boyfriend
so no messy emotions would weigh me down –
over-burdened with betrayal as my soul was so early on.

By the time we met I was sixteen
and tired of guys who wanted to fuck or be friends –
I had "use me" stamped on my forehead
in invisible ink for any predator to read.

He was funny
and sweet
and a virgin…
and I wasn't…
any of those things.

By the glow of his stereo and Foreigner,
waiting for a girl like you,
I suffered through his clumsiness
and fell in love with
his laugh
and his curls
and his smell.

We were together through my parents'
moving to another province
and leaving me to finish my semester
and the looming separation when I went to Europe.

I was his everything up to the moment I wasn't,
which happened to coincide with
the moment when I went south
to cross a picket line to the clinic
while protesters called me a murderer.

By the time we were over
I was sixteen
and gutted

98

and he did not return my calls
or reply to my letters.

I fell in love with his
laugh
and his smile
and his hands.

I learned, once again, to close up –
roll up –
armadillo tough.
To hold in my shame and keep out his pain.

I cried for years on that day in March
when I learned to
walk tall, without him,
past those who
screamed
murderer
in my face.

By the time I was ok again,
I was...
almost fifty.

Sunningdale, Berkshire

Agatha Christie disappeared at 36. A note
in her house mentioned a vacation,
her car abandoned in a quarry indicated
otherwise — the hood up, the lights on,
an old drivers license, a fur coat and a bag
of clothes were inside. A thousand officers
and fifteen thousand volunteers searched
the countryside. Sir Arthur Conan Doyle
presented a glove of Christie's to a medium
in hopes that she could help. Dorothy L. Sayers
visited the crime scene. Biplanes flew overhead,
the rivers were dredged. Her husband, the prime
suspect, Archie Christie was having an affair
everyone knew about, his wife included.

A musician spotted Agatha 11 days later
at the Swan Hydropathic Hotel.
She had signed in using the last name
of her husband's lover as an alias.
Agatha herself rarely spoke of the period,
blaming the whole incident on a dream state.
Some cried publicity stunt, others thought
it was just a lesson in husband shaming.
The husband and his mistress claimed
attempted framing. Christie omitted
the period from her autobiography.

Laurie McKay

Before Darkness

Before darkness creeps into the garden,
before the mosquitos begin to dine,
we settle into our lounge chairs
to breathe and enjoy the time.

Fragrant bouquets of summer,
mix with the nearby herbs.
Sounds of children laughing,
playing undisturbed.

Leaf-filtered sunset hues,
cloudless blue above,
frame the gilded birds in flight,
singing songs of love.

Entwining fingers, holding hands,
love connects and courses through.
As the twilight turns into night,
the day lives past its due.

Dear Poetry,

You lied to me
You swore this would be easy
That you would be here
In my darkest hours
That I would find solace in your simple rhythm
Your joyful rhyme
Your melodious metaphor
Your stunning simile
But after 21 hours
You are like the lover
That will not leave
You want breakfast and cuddles
You want my full attention
For me it is just word porn now
You toy with me
I indulge you
But I get nothing in return
My back aches
My head pounds
Yet still you demand
I can barely think
But you want more
Much, much more
You want all of me
Until my brain shrivels
And my fingers flail about
You own me
You miserable miser of misery
Poetry
It will do you good they said
And now I stand on the street-corner
Begging the muses for a morsel
Anything to get me through
Poetry
Keep it away from your children
And your grandmother
It will do you no good

In the dead of night
When my eyes want to close
And turn it to prose
You poetry just badger
And command

A demanding lover
Until the bitter
caustic end

Leaving out eight lines unprecedented

A woman . . . she had not known of love before,
nor is she a romantic.
So she did not realize the start of a marathon,
when suddenly she was in the middle of it.
Her heart rocked about so abruptly,
causing her nerves to run wildly
and stopped at the mention of a man-figure.
Unbeknownst . . . her hand lunging forward though her effort failed her,
when he only existed for a millisecond.

The Letter

Dear Grandchildren:
There is irony in that the
last thing you will ever forget
will be one of your firsts
crush
love
kiss
sex
broken heart
first to never be forgotten
first to stick with you
first to make you feel like that
first to make you hurt
first to make you feel alive

There is less irony
more fact
knowing that the firsts will
teach you the most
honor you the least
cause more discomfort
provide perspective
be impossible to explain to others
yet explain everything there is to know

These things I tell you
because they are true
because I know
because I care

Love,
Grandpa

P.S.
Don't tell your parents
you learned any of
this from me

Finding James

"Where's James?" They ask.
Every day, at least once,
"Do you know where James went?"
invades my thought process.

I sit next to him.
James, that is,
in a cramped space
once housing dinosaurs.

Old copy machines
generating too much heat
for two
side by side vents.

One directly over my head.
"Can you tell James I need him?"

"Are you kidding me?" I think,
"Of course," I smile.
I am a woman, after all,

Sitting in the first desk from the door.

James, the IT guy,
occupies the back cube,
a managerial impression
that has me viewed
as his God Damned Secretary!

I promptly forget
And move on with thoughts
of what x and y
max out to in the scheme of things.

"Have you seen James today?"

FUUUUUCK!
After six months here
is it not obvious?
I don't do James!

Focus

We focused on
The tide coming in
Our hair being doused
In rain
The house being a mess
Our ears ringing
In winter
The smell of plantains
Our hands holding books
In autumn
The sound of poetry
Our mouths shut
In readings
We focused
In readings
In autumn
In winter
In rain
To each other

Seema Kapur

Trusting

Trusting perception
getting into boiling water –
these potatoes are not cooked.

Leeam Frances Minas

The Night is for Sleeping

When was the last time,
you fell peacefully asleep at night

and not think about the things
that haunt your restless mind?

When was the last moment where you went to bed to sleep,
hugged your pillows so tight,

and did not worry about the monsters inside your head,
along with the problems that give you a fright?

When was the last time you lay down,
and felt surging relief after a tiring day,

and not stare at the ceiling in dread
while you think about the things that are gone but should've stayed?

When was the last time you cuddled
among warm blankets and your favorite stuffed bear,

and didn't wake in the middle of the night, screaming,
because of an unwanted nightmare?

When was the last time you slept
'till the early sunrise

and not stayed up all night,
thinking about your inevitable demise?

When was the last time you happily put off
everything that you are doing just so you could rest,

and not cry because of school work,
and all the things you need to review for your test?

When was the last time you have closed your eyes,
satisfied with how your day went,

and not painfully shut them,
while you ask what every crack in your heart meant?

When was the last time you looked forward
to going home,

and did not worry about how you'll end up wide awake in your bed feeling
all alone?

Just tonight, please hold tight.
Stop thinking, stop worrying.

Just stop what you are doing.
Give it to God, and go to sleep, Darling.

Flying Over Napa

Harness joins silk chute.
Breeze picks up as boat speeds up,
released into sky.
Serene, peaceful, floating high,
azure water shimmers teal!

Wet bikes whizz below,
dots speckled on azure rug.
Foam shoots fair satin,
strangely, perfectly silent.
Floating free, blissful warm air!

Golden sand contrasts;
jaded grass and trees colour.
Perfect picture plants,
so still, serene, sun-drenched view,
vision of falling deep, wet.

Truly living life!
The taste of salt, seaweed smells,
fish shadows below.
postcard images engraved,
never to be forgotten...

Poetries Thru Time Locked In Space

Unexpected twist and turn
A day a night interlocking
Meeting poets across the global field
In space and in time
In its high and its low points
Still a path of overcoming beyond
Cascading in every prompts
Collecting new experiences
Understanding a humanity
A humanity overshadowing
Taking flight in all circumstances
A jubilation in course of meeting things
Undocumented or otherwise stipulated
Humanity overcoming beyond its expectation

Glory, Poorly

Cows mooed as I held your trembling torso
through the seizures.
Your eyes reflected the moon when you came to;
I startled at my first womanly moment.
I knew I wanted to lay down, and stroke you breastbone to navel.

My fumbling reinforced your recovery.
You wouldn't let me be late.
That was your excuse.
I didn't have the emotional vocabulary to truck with your banter,
or you would have been my first
instead of, years later, a man who didn't know
what he was taking
under the canopy.

Our breath fogged in front of us
as we jogged back to your beat-up jeep
and rolled past the lake,
at once,
austere and serene.
You made me laugh, all the way home
but I felt your panic.

The porch light was on,
and you reached past me
to open my door.

An Early Dusk, An Early Dawn

Melancholic both,
  the Former, end of the day's unfulfilled dreams,
  the Latter is a new day to hope, on to another dream.

Diminishing nature's light,
turning on a new set of rays,
both dimly lit, both need eye adjustment.
The best time to think and ponder,
The best time to start the day right.

Melancholic both, yes.
Tho one is ending, the other is just beginning.
An Early Dusk, An Early Dawn.
One is a culmination, one is an onset.

Same panoramic view,
but Dusk is nostalgic, Dawn is inspiring.
Both gives one a sense of well-being.

An Early Dusk, An Early Dawn.
Likewise beautiful, likewise scenic.
Brings peace, serenity, tranquility,
To the perceptive One

Me....

Mr. Doubt

Doubt went on a trip to Arkansas,
he played around,
he thought *oh what a beautiful life
just to be free out in the light.*

Dreaming of a life so free
he ventured into the enchanted wood
to see how wonderful it would be.
He saw trees springing up,
birds chirping in trees.

Late evening came,
he said *oh no I am lost
how will I find my way.*
He saw a little hut
and went in for a peek.

It was well kept and neat.

he thought to himself,
just what I needed
so he went in to sleep.

The others wondered
Where is Mr. Doubt?
He was nowhere
to be found.

Lighthouse Keeper

They show up angry, hungry, afraid.
Missing their homes, missing their beds, needing their moms.
Some are defensive, some are shy, some tell tall tales.
Some even invent dangerous games, and revel in the chaos.
Yet you smile, you listen, you comfort.
Your touch calms, your voice reassures, your eyes pay attention.
The day twists and turns, yet you steer the ship through rough seas
with the expertise of a master mariner.
Adventures in science, history, art,
math, music, language and beyond, are laid at their feet.
Golden keys to open locked doors and secret passwords to hidden portals
unveiled and deciphered.
Missing books, broken pencils, empty cabinets
replenished and filled with portions of your meager paychecks.
Those designer shoes and exotic cruises to foreign lands
will have to wait,
while you spread magic,
share wisdom,
and create bright futures.

The Diner

I wandered in hoping to do some work,
I caught a glimpse of you,
my whole world churned.

Thirty years is a long time.
I just thought of you,
how is it you are now here?

I stepped back hoping you didn't notice,
I turned and ran into the streets.
Good thing you did not follow!

Strangers

Time mocked the strangers sitting on the bench, deep at night, bathed in lamp light, talking through the silence in between. In spite of knowing everything about each other, they were still strangers. Two strangers singing to the soft wind, smiling at the blinking stars, playing with the sleepless night.

And the weather grew old,
time weak, memory fragile,
strangers remain strange.

It was a bright sunny day. The stranger came to meet her. Shaking hands they became friends. A Stranger went away, in came a friend. He was kind, merry, a happy soul. He told her stories of past, present, and future. Yet she knew nothing about him. In spite of beings friends, they failed to find the true meaning. So she went into the past in search of her stranger.

Lost friends returned,
forgotten memories retold,
but not the stranger.

Ghost

"You can be a ghost
and I will not be scared.
Your coffin won't make me shiver.
Haunt me, I won't mind."
That is what he told me at the cliff edge.

I jumped into the abyss while he watched.
I flew into depths unknown to life. Again.

As I materialized behind him on the cliff edge
and prepared to push him down too,
I felt sorry for the weeping figure.
He hadn't known I was a ghost already.
Worse, he didn't know he was one too.

Paul Sanford

Denny's "America's Diner"

Kristen and I go there for privacy
to discuss the drama in the house,
to find a way to take back our home
from the lodgers we had invited in.
To plot the Revolution.

I always order, except when I don't,
The Everyday Slam (which sounds like a punk dance):
Whole-wheat pancakes,
Sugarless Syrup,
Scrambled eggs with steak sauce instead of ketchup,
just to class things up.
Sausage – not bacon.
Bacon isn't really food, I say,
to Kristen's annoyance.
She likes the taste of bacon
but won't let me get it for her.

Over the years we have seen the economy change;
The servers are newer hires who don't last as long as the veterans,
who moved on after their hours were cut
to avoid giving them bennies.
So nobody touches my shoulder and calls me "honey" any more.

Now the dramatic couple and their sweet teenager are gone,
replaced by a quiet, amiable fellow.
The house is quiet.
We eat at home more,
especially since my blood sugar edged up.
I no longer eat pancakes.

Denny's, "America's Diner."
Somehow we caught on
the food wasn't that great;
nor the service
nor the atmosphere.
It was the company we kept all along.

Fable of a Fairy Tale

Aesop's fox, Goldilocks' Papa Bear,
& Little Red — striding through 60's
suburbia in strident Soviet sunshine.

Cinderella has run away to the city (again)
& they seek to bring her home (yet again)
even though they know she won't want to,

no one's sure what the moral here is or what
archetype they each are forced to portray,
but they know it will all resolve in the end.

in these kind of tales, it usually does. Three
characters on a mission in the Western sun.

Memengwaa

She lived in East Vancouver,
or, Edmonton, or, Winnipeg, or, Toronto.
She left the Rez when at thirteen,
she was young, thin, beautiful and battered.
It's said she met the pig farmer once,
but to this day no one knows that for sure.
She was last seen in two thousand and twelve,
in a needle exchange shop in B.C.
She asked if she could get needles for a friend.
Alberta was cold on January 5th,
the baby's untimely reception even colder.
Daddy was dead, frozen in a field,
the family claims it was the police, no one knows.
Mommy was addicted to crack, as too the baby,
the child lost a child at twelve.
A picture shows a smile and dark eyes to adore,
There are only two and the second is blurry.
She left an unknown life to a life unknown.
Is she missing? Is she dead?
The question is, does anyone really care?

For the Guy at the Bar Whose Name I Didn't Catch

Like most things,
you've lost your charm,
but keep smiling
and I'll go home
with you anyway.
Or at least to your
car where we'll
fog the windows
and smoke
your last cigarette.

The Connection

Dear Corporation,

The rains have outperformed themselves this year.
They showered their blessings on us and the roads with
their torrential downpour and incessant affection.
As a consequence, they washed away the fragile tar
on the roads, that you had carefully prepared just
for this season.

The muddy rainwater fills these broken patches.
Walking on these roads is like learning to walk again,
with careful steps. The vehicles have a gala time,
sloshing the water onto themselves and the passers-by.

The passengers inside the vehicles experience what
the farmers using bullock-carts do, in their fields.
What a lovely way to unite people living in cities
with those in villages. Now, both experience the same
speed, the same jerks and the same movements.

Though miles apart, your intent to connect the diverse
lifestyles, with this common approach is commendable.

Yours sincerely,
The street users

Acknowledgments

A thank you is owed to all the contributors. I am so very grateful for your words.

Additional thanks are owed to Jacob Jans and J.I. Kleinberg for your editing help.

www.ingramcontent.com/pod-product-compliance
Lightning Source LLC
Chambersburg PA
CBHW021130020426
42331CB00005B/701